Law Enforcement

United States Marshals Service

by Michael Green

Consultant:
John J. Smith
Retired Inspector, U.S.M.S.
Retired U.S.M. Association

RiverFront Books

an imprint of Franklin Watts
A Division of Grolier Publishing
New York   London   Hong Kong   Sydney
Danbury, Connecticut

RiverFront Books
http://publishing.grolier.com
Copyright © 1999 Capstone Press. All rights reserved.
No part of this book may be reproduced without written permission from the publisher.
The publisher takes no responsibility for the use of any of the materials or methods
described in this book, nor for the products thereof.
Printed in the United States of America.
Published simultaneously in Canada.

Library of Congress Cataloging-in-Publication Data
Green, Michael, 1952–
    United States Marshals Service/by Michael Green.
    p. cm.—(Law enforcement)
    Includes bibliographical references (p. 45).
    Summary: An introduction to the United States Marshals Service, its
history, functions, responsibilities, officers, equipment, and targeted criminals.
    ISBN 0-7368-0189-8
    1. United States. Marshals Service—Juvenile literature. [1. United States.
Marshals Service. 2. Occupations.] I. Title. II. Series: Green, Michael, 1952–
Law enforcement.
HV 8144.M37 G74 1999
363.28'2'0973—dc21

                                                           98-46131
                                                           CIP
                                                           AC

Editorial Credits

Connie R. Colwell, editor; Timothy Halldin, cover designer; Kimberly Danger
and Sheri Gosewisch, photo researchers

Photo Credits

Corbis, 15, 17, 23
International Stock/Ron Sanford, 21
Uniphoto/Mark Reinstein, 37, 38
U.S. Marshals Service, cover, 4, 7, 8, 10, 12, 19, 25, 26, 28, 30, 32, 34, 41, 42-
43

Table of Contents

Chapter 1

The U.S. Marshals Service

The U.S. Marshals Service is a federal law enforcement agency. Federal law enforcement agencies make sure that federal laws are obeyed. Federal laws are the orders of federal judges, Congress, the attorney general, and the president of the United States. The U.S. Marshals Service is the oldest federal law enforcement agency in the United States.

U.S. Marshals and Deputy U.S. Marshals make up the U.S. Marshals Service. Marshals are selected by the president. Deputy marshals are hired by the Justice Department. Marshals and deputy marshals work together to enforce federal laws.

The U.S. Marshals Service is the oldest federal law enforcement agency in the United States.

Catching Fugitives

One duty of the U.S. Marshals Service is to catch federal fugitives. Some fugitives are criminals who have escaped from jail. Others are crime suspects who refuse to appear in federal courts. The suspects need to appear before judges and juries. These people decide if the charges against the suspects are true. Each year, the Marshals Service arrests more than 19,000 federal fugitives.

The Marshals Service sometimes needs help to catch federal fugitives. State and local police agencies work with the Marshals Service to catch these fugitives. Police agencies around the world also help the Marshals Service. For example, federal fugitives sometimes escape the country. The Marshals Service then asks police agencies in other countries to catch the fugitives.

Protecting the Federal Courts

The U.S. Marshals Service guards the federal courts. This keeps order and protects all people in federal courtrooms. This helps the federal courts run smoothly.

The U.S. Marshals Service guards the federal courts.

Federal judges often need protection from suspects. Suspects may try to hurt judges in courtrooms. They even may try to hurt judges outside courtrooms. The Marshals Service protects federal judges. It will guard judges' homes all day and night if necessary. The Marshals Service protects more than 2,000 federal judges.

The U.S. Marshals Service protects federal witnesses.

Not only judges need protection in federal courts. Citizens who testify against suspects also need protection. The Marshals Service protects these witnesses during trials.

Witness Security Program

Sometimes witnesses need special protection. The U.S. Marshals Service gives these witnesses new names and safe places to live. This is called the Witness Security Program.

The Marshals Service also protects the families of witnesses in the Witness Security Program. The Marshals Service gives the family members new names. They help witnesses and their families find housing, schooling, and jobs. They also teach witnesses and their families how to stay safe.

The Witness Security Program protects thousands of witnesses and their families. Since 1970, the Marshals Service provided nearly 7,000 witnesses with new identities. About 9,400 family members also have received new identities.

Securing Prisoners

The U.S. Marshals Service is responsible for federal prisoners. The Marshals Service helps manage more than 30,000 federal prisoners every day.

The Marshals Service is responsible for moving prisoners safely from place to place. Some prisoners must be moved to different jails. Others must appear in federal courts. Some prisoners need to be moved to hospitals. The Marshals Service transports more than 160,000 prisoners to these places every year.

Managing Property

The U.S. Marshals Service sometimes manages property. It controls property that has been forfeited to the U.S. government. This property must be given to the government. For example, some drug dealers buy and sell illegal drugs from houses or businesses. They may use cars or boats to ship these drugs. This property is forfeited to the government if the drug dealers are convicted.

The Marshals Service controls all forfeited property. This includes more than $1 billion in houses, apartment buildings, and businesses. It also includes cars, boats, and airplanes.

The Marshals Service sells the forfeited property to citizens at auctions. The money from the auctions belongs to the U.S. government. The government uses the money to enforce laws.

The U.S. Marshals Service controls forfeited property.

Chapter 2

History of the Marshals Service

The 13 colonies declared their independence from England after the Revolutionary War (1775–1783). Congress then created the federal court system. Congress selected judges to run these federal courts. Congress also created the offices of U.S. Marshal and Deputy U.S. Marshal to enforce the judges' orders. Since then, marshals and deputy marshals have taken part in many events in U.S. history.

Frederick Douglass was appointed U.S. Marshal of the District of Columbia in 1876.

The First Duties

George Washington hired the first group of U.S. Marshals in 1789. Washington hired one marshal for each of the 11 states. He also hired two more marshals for two areas that were not yet states. These areas later became Kentucky and Maine.

The first marshals managed the business matters of the federal courts. The marshals rented courtroom spaces and jails. They hired bailiffs to take charge of prisoners in court. The marshals even hired janitors to clean federal courtrooms.

Marshals also performed other duties not connected to law enforcement. These duties included taking the national census every 10 years. The census showed the number of people living in the United States. The marshals did this job until 1870. By 1880, the federal government created another group to take the census. This group was called the Bureau of the Census.

The Whiskey Rebellion

In early U.S. history, U.S. Marshals were the only federal government officials in most parts of the country. Many citizens in these areas did not

U.S. President George Washington hired the first 13 U.S. Marshals in 1789.

like government laws or federal court orders. These citizens sometimes disobeyed or protested the federal orders. Marshals and deputy marshals had to enforce federal laws. They sometimes had to handle angry citizens.

For example, the government wanted to tax whiskey in 1791. This tax raised money to pay for the Revolutionary War. Pennsylvania depended on money earned from making and selling whiskey. The citizens thought whiskey taxes would take too much of their money. Tax collectors came to collect the tax money from the citizens of Pennsylvania. This made some of the citizens angry. They did not give the money to the tax collectors. Instead, they attacked the tax collectors. The government called these angry citizens the Whiskey Rebels.

The government wanted to know why the citizens did not pay the whiskey tax. In 1794, a federal judge wrote an order telling 75 Whiskey Rebels to come to court. Marshal David Lenox delivered the court papers to the citizens.

The citizens refused to go to court. They became angry with Lenox. They attacked Lenox at his friends' house. Lenox's friends fought back. Five Whiskey Rebels died in the fight.

A short time later, 500 Whiskey Rebels took Lenox prisoner. Lenox escaped. President Washington then sent 13,000 soldiers to Pennsylvania to stop the citizens from fighting. The soldiers controlled the Whiskey Rebels and stopped the fighting.

Many citizens of Pennsylvania did not think they should have to go to court for not paying the whiskey tax.

Moving West

Millions of U.S. citizens moved to western states and territories in the late 1800s. Many moved to these areas for land and jobs. But some of the settlers were outlaws.

The West had few law enforcement agencies. Outlaws believed they could get rich quickly in the West. The outlaws robbed stagecoaches, banks, and trains. Some outlaws stole U.S. mail.

U.S. Marshals tried to arrest these outlaws. One famous outlaw murdered three deputy marshals. His name was Billy the Kid. Deputy Marshal Pat Garrett worked in New Mexico's Lincoln County. For three years, Garrett tried to capture Billy the Kid. In 1881, Garrett shot and killed Billy the Kid after the outlaw had escaped from jail.

Protecting the Indian Territory

In 1830, Congress passed the Indian Removal Act. This law forced five American Indian tribes to move west of the Mississippi River. These were the Cherokee, Choctaw, Chickasaw, Creek,

U.S. Marshals in the West tried to stop outlaws from robbing stagecoaches, banks, and trains.

and Seminole tribes. The U.S. government sent these tribes to the area that is now Oklahoma. Congress promised the American Indians no other people could enter the area. Many people referred to the area as the Indian Territory.

Settlers often crossed the Indian Territory on their way west. Many American Indians became angry with the settlers. They wanted to protect their land. The American Indians tried to force the settlers to leave the territory. The settlers fought the American Indians. Deputy U.S. Marshals tried to stop the settlers and the American Indians from fighting. But settlers and American Indians continued to fight for many years.

The Civil War

By 1860, slavery divided the nation. The Northern states had made slavery illegal. The Southern states wanted slavery to remain legal.

In 1860, South Carolina broke away from the United States. Ten other Southern states then broke away. These states formed a new nation called the Confederate States of America. The United States and the Confederate States could not agree about slavery. This led to the Civil War (1861–1865).

During the Civil War, U.S. Marshals in the Northern states had two main duties. Marshals arrested people who supported the Confederate

Settlers often crossed the land that belonged to the American Indians on their way west.

States. Marshals also seized the land of Confederate supporters.

The United States won the Civil War in 1865. Congress then passed new laws that gave rights to African Americans. In 1865, slavery was outlawed in the United States. In 1866, African Americans won the right to vote.

Protecting Voters

After the Civil War, many white southerners feared that African Americans would gain power. They did not want African Americans to vote in elections. U.S. Marshals protected African Americans in the South.

A group of former Confederate soldiers organized a secret group against African Americans. They called themselves the Ku Klux Klan (KKK). Members of the KKK tried to keep African Americans from voting in the South. But marshals guarded places where people went to vote in the South.

The federal government passed new laws to stop the KKK. These laws made it a crime to attack people because of their race or color. Marshals enforced these laws. Marshals arrested thousands of KKK members.

The Civil Rights Movement

In the early 1900s, many U.S. schools were segregated. This meant African American and white students could not attend the same

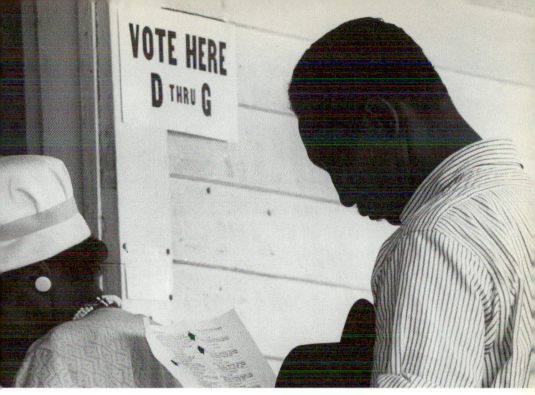

U.S. Marshals protected the first African American voters in the South.

schools. Many other businesses and public places were segregated as well. Some people wanted the government to pass laws to give rights to African Americans. They wanted all people to be treated equally. These people urged the government to pass such laws. This period is called the Civil Rights movement. U.S. Marshals enforced these civil rights laws.

In 1954, the U.S. Supreme Court ordered all U.S. schools to desegregate. This allowed African American and white students to attend the same schools. Many people were angry with this order. Some police officers in the South refused to enforce the order. They did not allow African American students in their communities to go to all-white schools.

The federal government ordered marshals to enforce desegregation. In 1962, an African American student named James Meredith tried to enroll in an all-white university in Mississippi. Many of the local white citizens did not want Meredith to enroll in the school. They started a riot. The marshals protected Meredith from this group of violent and uncontrollable citizens. But they could not stop the riot. The marshals were unable to enroll Meredith in the school.

U.S. Marshals escorted African American students to school during the Civil Rights movement.

President John F. Kennedy then sent soldiers to stop the fighting in Mississippi. The soldiers ended the riot and protected the marshals. The soldiers helped the marshals enroll Meredith in the university.

Chapter 3

Marshals and Deputy Marshals

Until the 1960s, U.S. Marshals and Deputy U.S. Marshals were not part of a national organization. Many marshals and deputy marshals did not like this. They wanted to earn more money. They also wanted to have more important duties. They thought their jobs should be more important.

A Need for Change

In the 1930s, U.S. Marshals and Deputy U.S. Marshals had few duties outside the federal courts. Marshals no longer enforced federal laws outside the courtroom. Other law enforcement officials such as police officers now performed these duties. Marshals could only guard federal

Lola Anderson Young was hired as a Deputy U.S. Marshal in 1919.

In 1969, the positions of U.S. Marshal and Deputy U.S. Marshal became the U.S. Marshals Service.

courts and deliver court papers. Deputy marshals worked mainly as bailiffs. These officials help judges in the courtrooms.

Marshals and deputy marshals did not receive much money for their jobs. For example, in 1937, some marshals earned only $1,800 each year.

People did not need special training to become deputy marshals. Many deputy marshals were retired police officers or soldiers. People who retire give up working their jobs because of their age.

Deputy marshals had little job security. Marshals hired their own deputy marshals. When the marshals left, the deputy marshals also lost their jobs.

A New Agency

In 1939, the Justice Department improved the job of Deputy U.S. Marshal. It set standards for all deputy marshals. They had to be between 23 and 50 years old. They had to be physically fit. They needed high school educations.

The Justice Department also made other changes. It allowed deputy marshals to stay even when the marshals who hired them quit.

In the 1960s, the Justice Department created a national headquarters in Washington, D.C. Officials at the headquarters created national standards. In 1969, the Justice Department grouped the positions of marshal and deputy marshal into one service. The two positions became the U.S. Marshals Service.

Chapter 4

Training

U.S. Marshals and Deputy U.S. Marshals need training to enforce federal laws. They must know and understand federal laws. They also must know how to operate their weapons. Marshals and deputy marshals go through difficult training before they can become a member of the U.S. Marshals Service.

Becoming a Deputy U.S. Marshal

Today, people who want to become Deputy U.S. Marshals must have certain qualities. They must be U.S. citizens between the ages of 21 and 37. They must be in excellent physical condition. They also must have college educations or training in law enforcement.

U.S. Marshals and Deputy U.S. Marshals need training to enforce federal laws.

Recruits at the Federal Law Enforcement Training Center (FLETC) learn to control prisoners.

People must apply to be deputy marshals. The Justice Department chooses some of these applicants to be recruits. The recruits must attend the Federal Law Enforcement Training Center (FLETC) in Glynco, Georgia. At FLETC, recruits must complete a tough 14-week training course.

Recruits study during their first eight weeks at FLETC. They study law enforcement. They learn how to solve crimes.

The recruits then have six weeks of physical training. They learn to search and control prisoners. They learn to search buildings and stop vehicles. The recruits who do well at FLETC become Deputy U.S. Marshals.

Becoming a U.S. Marshal

Most U.S. Marshals start out as law enforcement officials. Some start as deputy marshals. Others start as sheriffs or attorneys.

People who want to become marshals must have many skills. They must be good at dealing with people. They must know how to stay calm during emergencies. They also must know how to speak and write well.

The president of the United States appoints all U.S. Marshals. Senators tell the president about people in their communities who might make good marshals. The president then chooses one of these people to be the marshal for the community.

Chapter 5

Special Operations

The U.S. Marshals Service performs hundreds of special missions. It has a special group to perform these missions. This group is called the Special Operations Group (SOG).

The Special Operations Group

The SOG is a specially trained group of Deputy U.S. Marshals. The SOG is trained to handle national emergencies. A bomb threat is one kind of national emergency. A riot is another kind of national emergency.

The SOG has two programs that perform special missions. One is the Air Operations Branch. The other is the Missile Escort Program.

Members of the Special Operations Group (SOG) are trained to handle riots.

Air Operations Branch

The Air Operations Branch uses aircraft to perform special missions. This group is located in Oklahoma City.

The Air Operations Branch uses aircraft to help the SOG in many ways. It flies SOG teams to places where emergencies occur. It moves prisoners to jails or courts. It even moves some prisoners to other countries.

The Missile Escort Program

The Missile Escort Program helps the U.S. Air Force move missiles. The Air Force controls thousands of missiles. Sometimes it needs to move these missiles. The Missile Escort Program helps the Air Force escort the missiles. These Deputy U.S. Marshals guard the missiles while they are being moved.

The Missile Escort Program escorts two types of Air Force missiles. These types are the Minuteman missile and the cruise missile. The Air Force moves these missiles by truck.

Members of the SOG are specially trained to deal with the most dangerous missions.

The Missile Escort Program is responsible for the safety of the missiles. It guards the Minuteman and cruise missiles while they are being moved. It protects the Air Force trucks from attack. It also directs traffic around the Air Force trucks.

Chapter 6

Equipment and Safety

The U.S. Marshals Service uses a variety of equipment to enforce federal laws. Some of the equipment includes weapons, vehicles, and machinery. This equipment helps protect U.S. Marshals, Deputy U.S. Marshals, and others.

Weapons

The U.S. Marshals Service sometimes uses weapons to protect people. U.S. Marshals and Deputy U.S. Marshals carry guns when they guard the courts. They also carry guns when they escort prisoners. They use their guns only when they need to protect people or themselves from danger.

The U.S. Marshals Service uses weapons to protect themselves and others.

The deputy marshals in the SOG have special weapons because their missions are especially dangerous. SOG missions require weapons with more power. These weapons include handguns, rifles, and machine guns.

Vehicles

The U.S. Marshals Service moves prisoners in different vehicles. These include cars, vans, trucks, and buses. The Marshals Service sometimes uses planes for moving federal prisoners long distances. The Marshals Service has two large passenger jets and many smaller jets.

The Marshals Service guards the prisoners carefully while they are being moved. Prisoners need to be handcuffed while they ride in the vehicles. They also need to wear leg irons.

Machines

The U.S. Marshals Service often uses machines to help protect the federal courts. Suspects sometimes hide dangerous weapons in their clothes, briefcases, purses, or packages. X-ray machines and metal detectors help marshals find hidden

The U.S. Marshals Service uses x-ray machines and metal detectors to help protect federal courts.

weapons. X-ray machines take pictures through solid objects. Metal detectors beep when they are near metal. The Marshals Service finds thousands of weapons each year with the help of these machines.

The Marshals Service uses this equipment to perform its duties. The Marshals Service protects thousands of people every year.

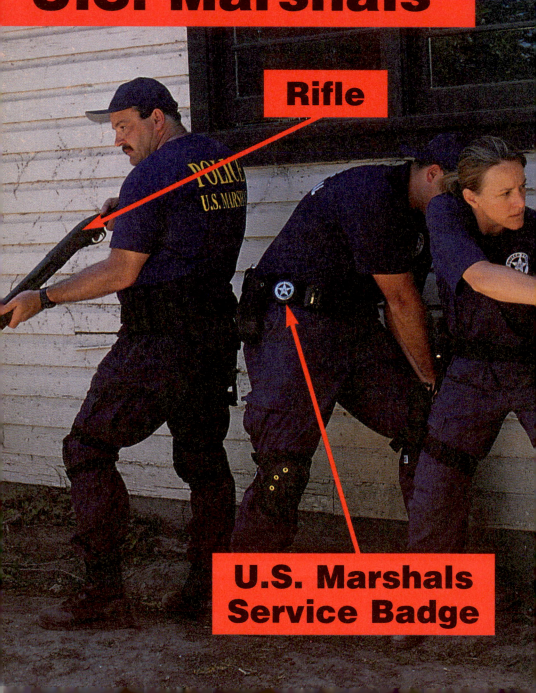

Deputy U.S. Marshals

Rifle

U.S. Marshals Service Badge

Handgun

Machine Gun

Words to Know

bailiff (BAY-lif)—an official who helps a judge in court

county (KOUN-tee)—a part of a state with its own local government

forfeit (FOR-fit)—to give up the right to something

fugitive (FYOO-juh-tiv)—someone who runs away from the police

investigate (in-VESS-tuh-gate)—to gather facts to discover who committed a crime

recruit (ri-KROOT)—someone who has recently joined an organization

segregate (SEG-ruh-gate)—to keep people of different races apart

seize (SEEZ)—to arrest or take something; the U.S. Marshals Service sometimes seizes the property of drug dealers.

testify (TESS-tuh-fye)—to state facts in court

To Learn More

Cohen, Paul and Shari Cohen. *Careers in Law Enforcement and Security.* New York: Rosen Publishing Group, 1995.

Green, Michael. *Bomb Detection Squads.* Law Enforcement. Mankato, Minn.: RiverFront Books, 1998.

Green, Michael. *SWAT Teams.* Law Enforcement. Mankato, Minn.: RiverFront Books, 1998.

Useful Addresses

National U.S. Marshals Museum
Wyoming Territorial Prison and Old West Park
975 Snowy Range Road
Laramie, WY 82070

Office of Congressional and Public Affairs
Office of Justice Programs
U.S. Department of Justice
810 Seventh Street
Washington, D.C. 20531

**U.S. Marshals Service Employment and
 Compensation Division**
Field Staffing Branch
600 Army Navy Drive
Arlington, VA 22202-4210

U.S. Marshals Service Headquarters
Office of Public Affairs
600 Army Navy Drive, CS III
Arlington, VA 22202-4210

Internet Sites

U.S. Department of Justice
http://www.usdoj.gov/

U.S. Marshals Service
http://www.usdoj.gov/marshals/

Welcome to PoliceScanner.Com
http://www.policescanner.com

Index